365 Quotes and Meditations

Business and Politics

VICTOR DE LA FUENTE

365 Quotes and Meditations
BUSINESS AND POLITICS

Víctor de la Fuente

Copyright © 2018 Víctor de la Fuente

All rights reserved. No part of this publication may be reproduced, distributed, or transmitted in any form or by any means, including photocopying, recording, or other electronic or mechanical methods, without the prior written permission of the publisher, except in the case of brief quotations embodied in critical reviews and certain other noncommercial uses permitted by copyright law.

365 Quotes and Meditations – Motivation/ Víctor de la Fuente. – 1st Edition

ISBN 978-1729075050

Index

PROLOGUE

THE QUOTES. THE INSPIRATION.

ABOUT THE AUTHOR

OTHER BOOKS BY THE AUTHOR

Prologue

Since my early adulthood, I collected phrases and concepts that awakened "something" in me really caught my attention. Sometimes it was simple curiosity. Others created a seed that in time would mold a way of thinking, values or an ideology. This collection is a selection of quotes, concepts, aphorisms, reflections and arguments that marked me in one way or another.

In the collection, I mostly include modern authors. That way I avoid overused classic phrases from writers, thinkers and personalities. This isn't a mass-produced book as a result of copying/pasting the most famous quotes. Paradoxically, this is a very personal book, even though not all words are mine and I speak through others. The book contains modern philosophy based on modern philosophers, essays in a wide range of themes, and even fiction and pop culture, too. In some cases, the quote has no author. In those cases, it's mostly because there's no assignable author and because the quotes are my own reaping both in their whole originality and their adaptation.

Among the different volumes of the collection, no quote is repeated so, even when there are common and comparable lessons among topics, there's no repeated quote and therefore, original and unique material in each volume.

There are many ways to enjoy the following pages. One of the options is to read a quote each day, take it in and reflect on that concept. Another option would be to work each phrase particularly, taking advantage of the space between one another for annotations and personal reflections. And finally, all at once. Depending on the objective that each person has, they will take more or less advantage one way or another.

In any case, in order to internalize the concepts, repetition is key. Precisely with that goal in mind, concepts are referenced in different ways all along the book. Besides, an approach to a concept will awaken interest in some people in a way and attract others in another. At the same time, it shouldn't be a surprise when a concept is quoted different times proclaiming different philosophies. More with the intent to force the reflection rather than pleasing every public, this way we manage to test our beliefs while generating discussion, and probably confirm that there isn't a sole correct perception about determined topics.

It's hard to separate the "pseudo-" from revolutionary things. Even more to separate a superficial, instant gratification from a deeper thought. Without further ado, I invite the reader to get into the reflections that I hope will provoke them as much as they provoked me.

365 Quotes and Meditations

The quotes. The inspiration.

For each trend, there is a countertrend.

Patient for growth but impatient for profit.

Expertise without experimentation makes you predictable. Experimentation without expertise is random success.

The virtuous worry about their integrity, lesser humans about their reputation.

Nassim Nicholas Taleb

Pay is not a retrospective reward for merit but a prospective incentive for contributing to production.

></a> Thomas Sowell

> Book: Economic fallacies and facts

You can acquire a lot in life, if you are prepared to give up a lot to get it.

> Bruce Lee

> Book: Striking thoughts

In trying to take all the risk on to yourself, you're actually increasing the risk to all of us.

> Parks

> Book: The girl with all gifts

The long-term failure of short-term thinking.

Specialization tends to limit the field of problems that the specialist is concerned with.

Joseph Campbell

Book: The power of myth

The problem isn't Madoff; the problem is what pushed him into doing it.

Slavoj Zizek

Book: Demanding the impossible

You are the best investment you'll ever make.

Talent must be stimulated by facts and ideas. Do research.

Book: Story: Substance, Structure, Style, and the Principles of Screenwriting

Where time is money, it is governed by the usual rules of economics. We wait for what we value. [...] When demand overwhelms supply, waiting time may exceed the original value of the product itself.

Never outsource the future.

Full vs marginal thinking.

Because failure is often at the end of a path of marginal thinking, we end up paying for the full cost of our decisions.

You don't signal competence if you don't take risks for it-there are few such low-risk strategies.

Nassim Nicholas Taleb

Book: Skin the game

Until people realize that they are talking in a circle, however large that circle may be, they may continue to believe insinuations that give tautologies their power, as if they were conclusions about the external world instead of arbitrary definitions inside their own heads.

Thomas Sowell

Book: Economic fallacies and facts

You have to live the solution, and to set about solving the new problems that this creates.

David Deutsch

Book: The beginning of infinity

The winner's curse. When many bidders compete for the same object, the winner of the auction is often the bidder who most overvalues the object being sold.

Richard H. Thaler

Book: Misbehaving

Why do people gamble when most people consistently lose?

Success can kill you just as failure can.

David Lynch

Book: Catching the big fish

Growth for the shake of growth is the ideology of the cancer cell.

Extraordinary success is sequential, not simultaneous.

> Gary Keller
>
> Book: The ONE thing

It is very easy to confuse superior performance with the results you would expect from luck.

> Michael J. Mauboussin
>
> Book: The success equation

Nobody laughs if it works.

> Gabe in Sam Sheridan
>
> Book: A fighter's heart

While a definitely optimistic future would need engineers to design underwater cities and settlements in space, and indefinitely optimistic future calls for more bankers and lawyers. Finance epitomizes indefinite thinking because it's the only way to make money when you have no idea how to create wealth.

> Peter Thiel
>
> Book: Zero to one

An indefinite world, people actually prefer unlimited optionality; money is more valuable than anything you could possibly do with it. Only in a definite future is money a means to an end, not the end itself.

> Peter Thiel
>
> Book: Zero to one

The importance of failure: a culture of false success.

Each company was obsessed with defeating its rival, precisely because there were no substantive differences to focus on.

> Peter Thiel
>
> Book: Zero to one

The explanation would not be about why they made mistakes -problems are inevitable- but why they failed to correct them.

David Deutsch

Book: The beginning of infinity

The plural of anecdote is not data.

Daniel J. Levitin

Book: Organized mind

Wanting fast motivates thinking fast.

What distinguishes experts from novices is that they know what to pay attention to and what to ignore.

Daniel J. Levitin

Book: Organized mind

Money and time are linked, but they are not equal.

The numbers have no way of speaking for themselves. We speak for them.

Nate Silver

Book: The signal and the noise

Complex language hides the lack of an interesting idea.

Overspecialization also is not a great idea. Consider what can happen to you if your job disappears completely.

Nassim Nicholas Taleb

Book: The black swan

When is a cost a loss?

Richard H. Thaler

Book: Misbehaving

'Payment depreciation,' meaning that the effects of sunk costs wear off over time.

Richard H. Thaler

Book: Misbehaving

The inverse problem of the rare events. To estimate a rare event you need a sample that is larger in inverse proportion to the occurrence of the event.

John Brockman

Book: Thinking: The New Science of Decision-Making

Shadow work-it represents a kind of parallel, shadow economy in which a lot of the service we expect from companies has been transferred to the customer.

Daniel J. Levitin

Book: Organized mind

Overoptimized to the point of maximal vulnerability.

John Brockman

Book: Thinking: The New Science of Decision-Making

Before we demand more of our data, we need to demand more of ourselves.

Nate Silver

Book: The signal and the noise

A difference between an error and a systematic error.

John Brockman

Book: Thinking: The New Science of Decision-Making

Impact bias: people tend to overestimate the impact of future events. That is, they predict that future events will have a more intense and more enduring hedonistic impact than they actually do.

John Brockman

Book: Thinking: The New Science of Decision-Making

Prediction is important because it connects subjective and objective reality.

Nate Silver

Book: The signal and the noise

When we do things randomly, we can expect random results.

To become over-familiar with one weapon is as much a fault as not knowing it sufficiently well.

Miyamoto Musashi

Book: The Book of Five Rings

The distinction between uncertainty and risk.

Nate Silver

Book: The signal and the noise

The key is in remembering that a model is a tool to help understand the complexities of the universe, and never a substitute for the universe itself.

Nate Silver

Book: The signal and the noise

The key is in determining whether the patterns represent noise or signal.

Nate Silver

Book: The signal and the noise

Ergodicity: it means, roughly, that (under certain conditions) very long sample paths would end up resembling each other.

Nassim Nicholas Taleb

Book: Fooled by randomness

Nobody accepts randomness in his own success, only his failure.

Nassim Nicholas Taleb

Book: Fooled by randomness

Data snooping: fitting the rule on the data.

Nassim Nicholas Taleb

Book: Fooled by randomness

It's not enough to be passionate yourself. You must also surround yourself with people who are passionate.

Carmine Gallo

Book: Talk like TED

Reasons hadn't created the decision; the decision had created them.

Book: Influence, The psychology of persuasion

Taking the money, wanting the money –proverbially or literally- makes you a servant to the people who have it. Indifference to it, turns the highest power into no power, at least as far as your life is concerned.

> Ryan Holiday
>
> Book: The daily stoic

Never engage in detailed overexplanations of why something important is important; one debases a principle by endlessly justifying it.

> Nassim Nicholas Taleb
>
> Book: Skin the game

'What' implies a specific response; if you ask yourself a question beginning with the word 'why', you can get many different answers, and they may all be correct.

> Syd Field
>
> Book: Screenplay

A constant state of distraction (what we euphemistically like to call multitasking).

Although the individual workers are fallible, systems and redundancies are usually in place, or should be, to ensure that no one person's momentary distraction or lack of organization brings everything to a grinding halt.

Daniel J. Levitin

Book: Organized mind

Satisficing is a tool for not wasting time on things that are not your highest priority. For your high-priority endeavors, the old-fashioned pursuit of excellence remains the right strategy.

Daniel J. Levitin

Book: Organized mind

The most crucial principles used by the attentional filter are change and importance.

Daniel J. Levitin

Book: Organized mind

Value in use (not in exchange).

There's always a larger, overaching question -the big target.

Jason

Book: Dark matter

If you survive until tomorrow, it could mean that either a- you are more likely to be immortal or b- that you are closer to death. Both conclusions rely on the exact same data.

Nassim Nicholas Taleb

Book: The black swan

To understand the future to the point of being able to predict it, you need to incorporate elements from this future itself.

Nassim Nicholas Taleb

Book: The black swan

You have to know exactly what they want and exactly what they're thinking, so that you can give them what you want them to have.

Mark Crispin Miller

Doc: Frontline: Merchants of cool

But infinite growth collides with finite energy.

When Plan A fails, you should have a Plan B, not Plan A recycled.

Andre Drazen

TV-Series: 24 hours

One considered, calculated move can be better than twenty reactive moves, no matter how well-executed they are. And that requires focus.

Captain America

Comic: Spiderman - The Other

Nothing is impossible, Mr. Angier. What you want is simply expensive.

Nikola Tesla

Movie: The Prestige

Succeed on your terms, not theirs.

Clarence

TV-Series: Boston Legal

People always wandering what the differences is between a warning and example. Differences is rather simple. Most people don't hit warnings, but they learn from examples.

Shadowman

TV-Series: Day Break

Nikola Tesla: Have you considered the cost of such a machine?

Robert Angier: Price is not an object.

Nikola Tesla: Yes, but have you considered the *cost*?

Movie: The Prestige

Integrity is the shield to greed and vanity.

Del Rio

TV-Series: Ozark

Doing too much also betrays an untrustworthy overabundance of effort.

Frank Hauser
Book: Notes on directing

Big enough to matter. Small enough to solve.

Dystopic instantiation of consumer capitalism.

Book: Addicted by design

If the product is unnecessary, like an iPad, there is a great chance the customer will become a fanboy because he had to choose to spend a big chunk of money on it. It's the choosing of one thing over another that leads to narratives about why you did it, which usually tie in to you self-image.

Book: The Power of Now

f it's what you want to hear, I think you already made up your mind.

> Nick
>
> Movie: Before we go

The more overdue a disruption is, the more sudden it is when it finally occurs, and the more off-guard the incumbents are caught.

In our winner-take-all society, fewer people will be big winners.

> Edward Russo
>
> Book: Winning decisions

People who are not morally independent tend to fit ethics to their profession (with a minimum spinning), rather than find a profession that fits their ethics.

> Nassim Nicholas Taleb

Book: Skin the game

The mere presence of an assistant suspends your natural filtering -and its absence forces you to do only things you enjoy, and progressively steer your life that way.

Nassim Nicholas Taleb

Book: Skin the game

Much time is wasted in meetings and deliberations because people focus on the wrong issues.

Edward Russo

Book: Winning decisions

Start small, become consistent, and increase at a manageable pace. That's how you optimize for the finish line, rather than the starting line.

Tynan

Book: Superhuman by habit

Objectives help you determine what information to seek.

John Hammond

Book: Smart choices

All they do is betray their lack of analysis.

Slavoj Zizek

Book: Demanding the impossible

Globalization does not mean we will all eat hamburgers; globalization means that a true global field will emerge.

Slavoj Zizek

Book: Demanding the impossible

Debt is an instrument to control and regulate the debtor, and, as such, it strives for its own expanded reproduction.

Slavoj Zizek

Book: Less than nothing

Time is just as important as the size of your sample.

Michael J. Mauboussin

Book: The success equation

Intuition works when the environment is stable and an individual has the opportunity to spend a great deal of time learning about it.

Michael J. Mauboussin

Book: The success equation

Optimization in a changing system is a setup for failure.

Michael J. Mauboussin

Book: The success equation

How predictable something is depends on what we are trying to predict, how far into the future, and under what circumstances.

Philip Tetlock

Book: Superforecasting

Like blind men arguing over the colors of the rainbow.

Rutkow in Philip Tetlock

Book: Superforecasting

The problem is that we move too fast from confusion and uncertainty to a clear and confident conclusion without spending any time in between.

Philip Tetlock

Book: Superforecasting

There is nothing mystical about an accurate intuition. It's pattern recognition.

Philip Tetlock

Book: Superforecasting

A forecast without a time frame is absurd.

Philip Tetlock

Book: Superforecasting

Scattered between those extremes. A phrase that looked informative was so vague as to be almost useless. Or perhaps it was worse than useless, as it had created dangerous misunderstandings.

Philip Tetlock

Book: Superforecasting

Aggregating the judgments of many people who know nothing produces a lot of nothing.

Philip Tetlock

Book: Superforecasting

Intuition can fail as spectacularly as it can work.

Philip Tetlock

Book: Superforecasting

Randomness and luck are related, but there is a useful distinction between the two. You can think of randomness as operating at the level of a system and luck operating at the level of the individual.

Business and Politics

Michael J. Mauboussin

Book: The success equation

Strategy paradox-situations where "the same behaviors and characteristics that maximize a firm's probability of notable success also maximize its probability of failure."

Michael J. Mauboussin

Book: The success equation

There is fear and insecurity in pride, for when one aims at being highly esteemed, and having achieved such status, he is automatically involved in the fear of losing one's status.

Bruce Lee

Book: Striking thoughts

Every creative decision must be made by choice, not necessity.

Syd Field

Book: Screenplay

Your lack of planning is not my emergency.

The stronger your point of view, the less competition you have. The more unique you are no one can compete with you.

Freedom is the liberty to choose our own constraints.

When I failed, if I failed, I'd fail quickly, so I'd have enough time, enough years, to implement all the hard-won lessons.

Phil Knight

Book: Shoe dog

If we're going to succeed, or fail, we should do so on our own terms, with our own ideas - our own brand.

> Phil Knight
>
> Book: Shoe dog

Knowing "when" enables you to perform "what" and "how" to your maximum potential.

> Michael Breus
>
> Book: The power of when

There is always a yearning to achieve more. I'll continue to climb, trying to reach the top but no one knows where the top is.

> Jiro
>
> Doc: Jiro Dreams of sushi

The calculation of enchantment.

Book: Addicted by design

From a minimalist point of view, employment should serve only two goals: funding that which allows you to live well and attaining fulfillment.

Danny Dover

Book: The minimalist mindset

Having an idea is not the same as knowing.

The goal is to reinforce for non-buyers the idea that BMW is a luxury brand. So BMW needs to advertise in media whose audience includes both rich and poor alike, so that the rich can see that the poor are being trained to appreciate BMW as a status symbol.

Kevin Simler and Robin Hanson

Book: The elephant in the brain

Discipline to decision making.

Edward Russo

Book: Winning decisions

No confuse the slogan with the idea.

Expensive things are expensive, not rare.

Sam Lustgarten

Book: Frugaling

Keeping free time scarce means people pay a lot more for convenience, gratification, and any other relief they can buy. It keeps them watching television, and its commercials. It keeps them unambitious outside of work.

Sam Lustgarten

Book: Frugaling

The high cost of not doing experiments.

Richard Nisbett

Book: Mindware

Take mistakes seriously, but never personally.

Daniel Coyle

Book: The little book of talent

Motivate the elephant.

Chip Heath and Dan Heath

Business and Politics

Book: Switch

There is a clear asymmetry between the scale of the problem and the scale of the solution. Big problem, small solution.

Chip Heath and Dan Heath

Book: Switch

In most cases, the cost of saying "I don't know" is higher than the cost of being wrong -at least for the individual.

Steven Levitt and Stephen Dubner

Book: Think like a freak

Results from today. Ideas for tomorrow.

Daniel Coyle

Book: The little book of talent

The key to learning is feedback.

> Steven Levitt and Stephen Dubner
>
> Book: Think like a freak

Debt is the illusion of success.

> Sam Lustgarten
>
> Book: Frugaling

Even if you are the best of the best, there is always a chance of failure.

> Elon Musk

Apply first principles analysis. Analogies are referencing the past.

Elon Musk

No one looks back at the end of their life and is happy about how many hours spent in meetings.

Danny Dover

Book: The minimalist mindset

␣t's not about the thing done. It's the beauty of the plan.

Farouk

TV-Series: Legion

Manufactured incalculability.

Book: Addicted by design

(About poker) when you win, it's always for the same reason. You might lose because you got unlucky, but you never win because of luck. The only way to win is to make better decisions than everyone else at the table.

Jonah Lehrer

Book: How we decide

Once inner success is achieved, there is less need for external victory. Let the external victory be the mere reflection of the triumph within.

Jerry Lynch

Book: Running within

Refuse to focus on anything but the joy and the fun of a well-executed plan.

Jerry Lynch

Book: Running within

What is one thing I can do that could make this better?

                                                                        Jason Selk

                                     Book: 10-Minutes Mental Toughness

To fail brilliantly.

The strategist makes small things into big things.

                                                      Miyamoto Musashi

                                       Book: The Book of Five Rings

Winning early and winning often.

If something is important enough you should try even if the probable outcome is failure.

Elon Musk

Redundancy as insurance.

Nassim Nicholas Taleb

Book: The black swan

Why predict something we can test?

Chip Heath

Book: Decisive

When our predictions and opinions clash with the universe's averages, the universe usually wins.

Chip Heath

Book: Decisive

They are products of history and community, of opportunity and legacy. Their success is not exceptional or mysterious. It is grounded in a web of advantages and inheritances, some deserved, some not, some earned, some just plain lucky -but all critical to making them who they are. The outlier, in the end, is not an outlier at all.

Malcolm Gladwell

Book: Outliers

Work is a prison sentence only if it does not have meaning.

Malcolm Gladwell

Book: Outliers

Exiting on top as, we like to think, geniuses invariably do.

Malcolm Gladwell

Book: Outliers

Accumulative advantage.

Malcolm Gladwell

Book: Outliers

When you are interested in something, the little things matter.

Todd Kashdan

Book: Curious?

What a product says about you is only important insofar as other people will notice your use of it. [...] Everyone must also know that everyone else knows it. [...] Everyone knows that everyone else is watching.

We are interested in actual value, not expected value.

Book: Football and philosophy

Now you know better, so you do better.

Marie Forleo

Book: Make every man want you

The privacy paradox: those who care the most about privacy are the ones with the least to hide.

Martin Varsavsky

Students are being prepared for a world that 'doesn't exist anymore.'

If something is "socially good," is it good for society, or merely seen as good by society?

Peter Thiel

Book: Zero to one

Politics must be about changing the world for the better and that means it is inherently pragmatic. A principle that can't be implemented is just a bad principle.

Julian Baggini

Book: The edge of reason

Unable to slow the mind-blogging pace of change, let alone to predict and control its direction, we focus on things we can, or believe we can, or are assured that we can influence: we try to calculate and minimize the risk that we personally, or those nearest and dearest to us at that moment, might fail victim to the uncounted and uncountable dangers which the opaque world and its uncertain future are suspected to hold in store for us. We seek to substitute targets on which to unload the surplus existential fear that has been barred from its natural outlets, and we find such makeshift targets making elaborate precautions against inhaling someone's else cigarette smoke, ingesting fatty foods, exposure to sun, or unprotected sex. Those who can afford it fortify ourselves against all visible and invisible, present or anticipated, known or as yet unfamiliar, diffuse but ubiquitous dangers through looking ourselves behind walls, driving armoured vehicles, wearing armoured clothing or taking martial art classes.

Zygmunt Bauman

Book: Liquid Modernity

A nation of one.

In the same way that the internet democratized information, virtual reality democratizes experiences.

This indignation is somewhat selective, since if we look at the world as a whole, many of those protesters are in the top 1 per cent and almost all are in the top 5 per cent.

Julian Baggini

Book: The big questions: ethics

Only progress is sustainable.

> David Deutsch
>
> Book: The beginning of infinity

People don't always make the best choices for themselves, so there's good reason to doubt whether they will always make the best choices for others.

Society composed only of narcissistic spectators. Everything is there solely for our enjoyment -- to view and be entertained by any means necessary.

If the only real responsibility were ultimate responsibility, then there could never be any responsibility at all, because everything that happens involves factors both within and outside of our control.

Julian Baggini

The finite is parochial. So there is no way of stopping there. The best explanation of anything eventually involves universality.

David Deutsch

Book: The beginning of infinity

The danger of this simplistic kind of relativism, which suspends judgment in the name of tolerance and pluralism.

Julian Baggini

Book: The big questions: ethics

For a rich person isolated from vertical socializing with the poor, the poor become something entirely theoretical, a textbook reference.

Nassim Nicholas Taleb

Book: Skin the game

Cultural values, inherited socially rather than biologically, may also reduce the statistical probability of advancing in income or occupations, even when the opportunity to do so is available -and no given individual chooses which culture to be born into.

Thomas Sowell

Book: Economic fallacies and facts

Who can be blamed for inheriting a culture that existed before they were born?

Thomas Sowell

Book: Economic fallacies and facts

Like every human, authority is imperfect and subject to abuse, so it cannot be unlimited - and it is not. But to invoke the blanket slogan "Question Authority" is to raise the question: By what authority do you tell us to question authority?

Thomas Sowell

Book: The quest for cosmic justice

Free choice implies full information.

If one is surrounded and pressed by millions of people, to prevent them from constantly impinging on you, the only way to do this is to ignore them as often as possible. Indifference to one's neighbor and his troubles is a conditioned reflex in life in NYC as it is in other big cities.

Book: Influence The Psychology of Persuasion

Charity takes care of an immediate need, where philanthropy tries to solve a problem.

A person who is more informed and educated has more capacity to make choices for herself, and therefore has more developed free will.

Julian Baggini
Book: Freedom Regained

That's why history is written by the victors, but it's victims who write the memoirs.

Carol Travis
Book: Mistakes were made

Stupidity originates in two distinct, even opposite sources, one scarcity; the other wealth. The poor can't afford to think wisely about the long term and the rich needn't bother.

The rich becoming sloppy thinkers, justifying anything they want to believe because they can afford to.

In a system there are no side effects -just effects, anticipated or not.

Daniel Goleman

Book: Focus: The Hidden Driver of Excellence

How could the conquerors have conquered in the first place, unless there were significant differences beforehand -whether economic, military, or whatever -between them and the conquered?

Thomas Sowell

Book: Economic fallacies and facts

There is a way to be free in an oppressive society and there is a way to be a slave in a free society.

William Geld

Movie: Code 46

Violence isn't always necessary, but it is always available.

This is how Liberty dies - with thunderous applause.

Senadora Amidala

Movie: SW E3 - Revenge of the Sith

The ethical way is always more robust than the legal. Over time, it is the legal that should converge to the ethical, never the reverse.

>Nassim Nicholas Taleb
>
>Book: Skin the game

Freedom is never free.

>Nassim Nicholas Taleb
>
>Book: Skin the game

Freedom entails risk -real skin in the game. Freedom is never free.

>Nassim Nicholas Taleb
>
>Book: Skin the game

Laws come and go, ethics stay.

Nassim Nicholas Taleb

Book: Skin the game

It is the most intolerant person who imposes virtue on others precisely because of that intolerance.

Nassim Nicholas Taleb

Book: Skin the game

Non mihi non tibi, sed nobis. Neither mine nor yours, but ours.

Nassim Nicholas Taleb

Book: Skin the game

Morality is higher authority than the law.

Julian Baggini

Book: The pig that wants to be eaten

The real revolution, for me, is when you change the balance itself: the measure of balance.

Slavoj Zizek

Book: Demanding the impossible

Where there is diversity there can be no identity.

Slavoj Zizek

Book: Less than nothing

It is much more satisfying to sacrifice oneself for the poor victim than to enable the other to lose the status of a victim, and perhaps become even more successful than ourselves...

Slavoj Zizek

Book: Event

A sign of ethical progress is the fact that torture is 'dogmatically' rejected as repulsive, without any need for further discussion.

Slavoj Zizek

Book: Event

If torture was always going on, why are those in power now telling us about it openly? There is only one answer: to normalize.

Slavoj Zizek

Book: Event

Attempts to account for freedom as a higher-level property "emerging" out of the complex interaction of lower-level elements which are part of a determinist network—the problem is then to determine what the status of freedom is if the same process which, at this higher level (the level of what Dennett calls "design"), involves freedom, can also be described at the lower level of its constituent elements in deterministic terms.

Slavoj Zizek

Book: Less than nothing

Stability today, it means the stability of dynamic development.

Slavoj Zizek

Book: Demanding the impossible

The paradox of an increasingly local politics in a world increasingly shaped and reshaped by global processes.

Zygmunt Bauman

Book: Liquid Modernity

Who speaks for planet earth? Our best tool is science and mathematics.

Patriotism and nationalism are the easiest ways to construct a shared sense of safety but they're also the least stable. The most promising kind of unity is one which is achieved. A unity that is an outcome of, not a prior condition to, shared life.

Society is ill if it stops questioning itself.

>Zygmunt Bauman
>
>Book: Liquid Modernity

In reality, most income is not distributed, so the fashionable metaphor of "income distribution" is misleading. Most income is earned by the production of goods and services. and how much production is "really" worth is a question that need not be left for third parties to determine, since those who directly receive the benefits of that production know better than anyone else how much that production is worth to them -and have the most incentives to seek alternative ways of getting that production as inexpensively as possible.

>Thomas Sowell
>
>Book: Economic fallacies and facts

Despite the popularity of the phrase "income distribution," most income is earned -not distributed.

>Thomas Sowell
>
>Book: Economic fallacies and facts

Neutral, in the face of injustice is on the side of the oppressor.

Wednesday

TV-Series: American Gods

Society, in disregard of the consequences for society as a whole, what is called "social justice" might more accurately be called anti-social justice, since what consistently gets ignored or dismissed are precisely the costs to society.

Thomas Sowell

Book: The quest for cosmic justice

Merit justifications for income and wealth differences are also fundamentally different from productivity justifications, even though the two are often confused.

Thomas Sowell

Book: The quest for cosmic justice

No conceivable redistribution of income, wealth, or other benefits will satisfy everyone, so there is no logical or political stopping-point in the process. Therefore the question is not which particular distribution is better or best, but whether the benefits of setting in motion a never-ending quest offers more potential for good or ill.

Thomas Sowell

Book: The quest for cosmic justice

We've lost the idea that politics is the means to build consensus and an opportunity to participate in something larger than ourselves.

'Sustain' is an interestingly ambiguous word. It can mean providing someone with what they need. But it also mean preventing things from changing -which can be almost the opposite meaning, for the suppression of change is seldom what human beings need.

David Deutsch

Book: The beginning of infinity

What are the reasons behind these disparities? Perhaps a more fundamental question might be: What reason was there to expect these groups to be the same in the first place?

Thomas Sowell

Book: Economic fallacies and facts

To take a radically different view of what the basic 'unit of value' is.

Julian Baggini

Book: What's it all about?

War is a matter of detail.

George Friedman

Book: The next 100 years

The even more conspicuous mark of our time is in the intense production of meaning and identity: my neighborhood, my community, my city, my school, my tree, my river, my beach, my peace, my environment. 'Defenceless against the global whirlwind, people stick themselves'. And let me note that the more they 'stick themlseves', the more defenceless against the 'global whirlwind' they become, and so also less capable of deciding, let alone asserting, the local, ostensibly their own, meaning and identities -to the great joy of global operators, who have no reason to fear the defenceless.

Zygmunt Bauman

Book: Liquid Modernity

The United States doesn't need to win wars. It needs to simply disrupt things so the other side can't build up sufficient strength to challenge it.

George Friedman

Book: The next 100 years

The essence of barbarism is the reduction of culture to a simple, driving force that will tolerate no diversion or competition.

George Friedman

Book: The next 100 years

The more precise weapons are, the fewer have to be fired.

George Friedman

Book: The next 100 years

To understand war, you need to understand more than the reasons a war was fought.

George Friedman

Book: The next 100 years

The devastation of the enemy, no matter how satisfying, is not the best strategy.

George Friedman

Book: The next 100 years

Imbalance of power.

George Friedman

Book: The next 100 years

To consider what the word basic in the phrase basic needs actually means.

Todd Kashdan

Book: The upside of your dark side

Robotics differs from all prior technologies in a fundamental way. Prior technologies have had labor displacement as a byproduct. Robotics is designed explicitly for labor displacement.

George Friedman

Book: The next 100 years

Civilized people fight selectively but effectively.

George Friedman

Book: The next 100 years

The goal of these interventions was never to achieve something -whatever the political rhetoric might have said- but to prevent something.

Here is the irony: Europe dominated the world, but it failed to dominate itself.

George Friedman

Book: The next 100 years

The United States tends to be careless in how it exercises its power globally. It's not stupid. It simply doesn't need to be more careful -in fact, being more careful could often reduce its efficiency.

George Friedman

Book: The next 100 years

The most brilliant leader of Iceland will never turn it into a world power, while the stupidest leader of Rome at its height could not undermine Rome's fundamental power.

George Friedman

Book: The next 100 years

Wars -when your country isn't destroyed- stimulate economic growth.

George Friedman

Book: The next 100 years

A commitment to the good of the species does not entail a commitment to one's own welfare.

Julian Baggini

Book: What's it all about?

If politics is a performance, then our audience is mostly our peers -friends and family- but others among us may be more interested in appearing smart than loyal.

Kevin Simler and Robin

Hanson Book: The elephant in the brain

Our institutions do end up achieving many of their official, stated goals, but they're often rather inefficient because they're simultaneously serving purposes no one is eager to acknowledge.

Kevin Simler and Robin
Hanson Book: The elephant in the brain

A nation is not a separate entity 'over and above' its citizen and territory but it is nevertheless distinguishable from them.

Julian Baggini
Book: What's it all about?

On 'the good of the species' view, it is not individuals that should be helped but a different kind of entity altogether: 'the species'.

Julian Baggini
Book: What's it all about?

The power of the unpredictable.

Proximity to power deludes some into believing they wield it.

Frank Underwood

TV-Series: House of Cards

More-perfect-than-perfect.

Free agent.

Paralysis by analysis.

The unstated assumption 'we know everything we need to'.

Daniel Goleman

Book: Focus: The Hidden Driver of Excellence

The focus dividend: the positive outcome of scarcity capturing the mind (ex. when time is short, you get more out of it).

Sendhil Mullainathan

Book: Scarcity

Procrastination is a thief. It steals, our time, our potential, our self-steem, our peace of mind.

Joyce Meyer

Book: Making Good Habits, Breaking Bad Habits

The rich live behind gates, not just to protect themselves, but to pretend to not need anyone else, if only for a moment.

Jaron Lanier

Book: Who owns the future

You must train day and night in order to make decisions.

Miyamoto Musashi

Book: The Book of Five Rings

Failure isn't the same thing as losing. Success isn't equivalent to winning.

You'll never go wrong leading by example.

The problem is that complex situations contain multiple causes for each effect. Yet we often want the simple 1-2 word answer. Yet most of the problems are not mechanical. They are not determinate. There is not a single cause. We live in a multi-cause, indeterminate world and our attempts to understand why events occurred will usually be frustrating.

If you want to lead the people, you must learn how to follow them.

Lao Tzu

Book: Tao Te Ching

Their problem is not your problem.

Greg McKeown

Book: Essentialism

Losing means you lost focus.

Greg McKeown

Book: Essentialism

Jootsing. Jumping out of the system.

Daniel C. Dennett

Book: Intuition pumps and other tools of thinking.

It's an entire industry that overglorifies data, because data is so easy to game, and the true data is so hard to obtain.

Brad

Business and Politics

Book Flash boys

How pro can you go?

Herbert Simon

Book: Manage Your Day-to-Day

What we say and what we imply.

Macroscopic harmony and microscopic individualism.

Kevin Dutton

Book: Wisdom of psychopaths

Expect obstacles.

Alex Lickerman

Book: The Undefeated Mind

Adversity as a catalyst.

Alex Lickerman

Book: The Undefeated Mind

The irony of the dandelion is this: The more failure the plants encounter corresponds strongly to the more success that the plants encounter.

The irony is that by being less focused on your results, you may achieve better ones.

Nate Silver

Book: The signal and the noise

The volume of information is increasing exponentially. But relatively little of this information is useful.

Nate Silver

Book: The signal and the noise

When we are making predictions, we need a balance between curiosity and skepticism. They can be compatible.

Nate Silver

Book: The signal and the noise

Focusing too much on the results and not enough on the correct decision-making process.

Nate Silver

Book: The signal and the noise

Kolgomorov complexity theory: something is random when you cannot explain how to derive a sequence using any fewer than the number of elements in the sequence itself.

Daniel J. Levitin

Book: Organized mind

Do not spend more time on a decision than it's worth.

Daniel J. Levitin

Book: Organized mind

It is easier for the rich to get richer, for the famous to become more famous.

Nassim Nicholas Taleb

Book: The black swan

The flips are independent of one another. The coin has no memory.

Nassim Nicholas Taleb

Book: The black swan

When winning leads to more winning.

Nassim Nicholas Taleb

Book: The black swan

More data means more information, perhaps, but it also means more false information.

Nassim Nicholas Taleb

Book: Antifragile

Size hurts you at times of stress.

>Nassim Nicholas Taleb
>
>Book: Antifragile

The more frequently you look at data, the more noise you are disproportionally likely to get.

>Nassim Nicholas Taleb
>
>Book: Antifragile

Excess wealth, if you don't need it, is a heavy burden.

>Nassim Nicholas Taleb
>
>Book: Antifragile

Wind blows the hardest the closer you get to the mountaintop.

> James Wesley
>
> TV-Series: Daredevil

The bigger picture perspective is crucial for understanding reality in its entirety.

More thinking is required.

> Mark Watney
>
> Book: The Martian

I guess you could call it a "failure", but I prefer the term "learning experience."

> Mark Watney
>
> Book: The Martian

The mistake of thinking that what is crucial is the mere quantity of a particular factor, rather than its quality.

> Julian Baggini
>
> Book: Freedom Regained

In Farther, like any continuous loop scenarios like thinner, or better, you gain value by measuring not from where you started, but from your last success.

The Pratfall effect: the occasional slip-up can enhance your likeability. However, it is important to realize that the effect only really works when you are in danger of being seen as too perfect.

> Richard Wiseman

Book: Think a little, change a lot

All of us are blind to whatever privileges life has handed us even if those privileges are temporary.

Carol Travis

Book: Mistakes were made

Every power can be misused.

Mihaly Csikszentmihaly

Book: Flow

Flags to replace altars.

Nassim Nicholas Taleb

Book: Antifragile

The competition of ideas.

>Mihaly Csikszentmihaly
>
>Book: The evolving self

The Planner and the Doer.

>Richard H. Thaler
>
>Book: Misbehaving

Smile and nod.

Value is a perception, not a calculation.

> Simon Sinek
> Book: Start with why

Success and achievement are not the same thing, yet too often we mistake one for the other.

> Simon Sinek
> Book: Start with why

Energy motivates but charisma inspires.

> Simon Sinek
> Book: Start with why

Gambling is very different from calculated risk.

> Simon Sinek
> Book: Start with why

Making decisions is a fundamental life skill.

John Hammond

Book: Smart choices

And yet there's a flip side to this drive to come together because for every "in" group, there are outsiders and the consequences of that can be very dark.

Slavoj Zizek

Doc: The brain with David Eagleman

One of the big problems of all great revolutionary movements of the 20th century, such as Russia, Cuba or China, is that they did change the social body but the egalitarian communist society was never realized. The dreams remained the old dreams and they turned into the ultimate nightmare. Now what remains of the radical left waits for a magical event when the true revolutionary agent will finally awaken. The depressing lesson of the last decades is that capitalism has been the true revolutionizing force. Even as it serves only itself.

Slavoj Zizek

Doc: The pervert's guide to ideology

Capitalism is all the time in crisis. This is precisely why it appears almost indestructible. Crisis is not its obstacle. It is what pushes it forwards, towards permanent self-revolutionizing, permanent extended self-reproduction, always new products.

> Slavoj Zizek
>
> Doc: The pervert's guide to ideology

The tension between deliberation and implementation.

> Philip Tetlock
>
> Book: Superforecasting

What comes after we solve the problem?

The future will be utopian, or there will be none.

Slavoj Zizek

Doc: The reality of the virtual

A thing done with moderation may later be judged to be insufficient. I have heard that when one thinks he has gone too far, he will not have erred.

Yamamoto Tsunetomo

Book: Hagakure

If one is but secure at the foundation, he will not be pained by departure from minor details or affairs that are contrary to expectation. But in the end, the details of a matter are important. The right and wrong of one's way of doing things are found in trivial matters.

Yamamoto Tsunetomo

Book: Hagakure

We ask "why is he rich (or poor)?" not "why isn't he richer (or poorer)?"; "why is the crisis so deep?" not "why isn't it deeper?"

Business and Politics

Nicholas Nassim Taleb

Book: The bed of Procrustes

Decision and action must be simultaneous.

Alan Watts

Book: The way of Zen

Win with something overwhelming, leave nothing to chance.

Sam Sheridan

Book: A fighter's heart

Moving first is a tactic, not a goal.

Peter Thiel

Book: Zero to one

Shifting your paradigm.

>Stephen R Covey
>
>Book: The 7 habits of highly effective people

Without a plan, we have no way of knowing. There's no real sense of urgency, no reason to seize the opportunity, and no sense that might lose it if we don't.

>Michael Hyatt and Daniel Harvaky
>
>Book: Living forward

If you aren't good at something, work harder, work smarter.

>Darren Hardy
>
>Book: The compound effect

The cost of waiting.

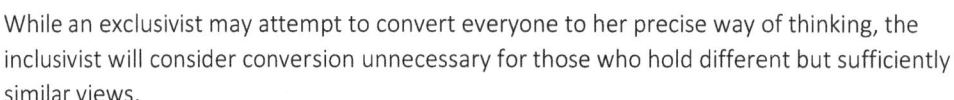

Jeff Olson

Book: The slight edge

While an exclusivist may attempt to convert everyone to her precise way of thinking, the inclusivist will consider conversion unnecessary for those who hold different but sufficiently similar views.

Jason Holt

Book: The ultimate Daily Show and philosophy

The principal biases of television news are not political at all. Rather, "the bias of the mainstream media is toward sensationalism, conflict and laziness".

Wallace in Jason Holt

Book: The ultimate Daily Show and philosophy

A problem worth solving.

Fear is a bad advisor.

Angela Merkel in Ryan Holiday

Book: Ego is the enemy

An idea is not enough.

Ryan Holiday

Book: Ego is the enemy

Capitalism is structurally always in crisis -this is why it is expanding all the time: it can only reproduce itself by way of 'borrowing from the future': by way of escaping into the future.

Slavoj Zizek

Book: The plague of fantasies

The ultimate "true" product would be the one which would not need any supplement, the one which would simply fully deliver what it promises -"you get what you paid for, neither less or more."

Slavoj Zizek

Book: The puppet and the dwarf

Decisions are temporary.

Jason Fried

Book: Rework

Without pluralism, democracy is the tyranny of the majority; but without democracy, pluralism is benign dictatorship.

Julian Baggini

Book: The edge of reason

In an age when all the grand ideas have lost credibility, fear of a phantom enemy is all the politicians have left to maintain their power.

Zygmunt Bauman

Book: Liquid Modernity

When a person is known by title, the attention is on a completed past, on a game already concluded, and not therefore to be played again. A title effectively takes a person out of play.

James Carse

Book: Finite and infinite games

By abstaining from vote, people effectively dissolve government –not only in the limited sense of overthrowing the existing government, but more radically. The vote of no confidence: it rejects the very frame of decision.

Slavoj Zizek

Book: Violence

Error of perception vs error of prediction.

When you forecast, make sure you forecast either the direction or the timing, but never both.

> Tan Liu
>
> Book: The ponzi factor

As efficiency increased, so did the standards that society came to expect.

All ideals suffer in the confrontation with reality.

> Deng Ming-Dao
>
> Book: Scholar warrior

The very idea of a nation is built on exclusion and defense.

Deng Ming-Dao

Book: Everyday Tao

Asap is implied. Everyone wants things done as soon as they can be done.

Jason Fried

Book: Rework

The map is not the territory. The representation is never the thing we are trying to represent.

Talent is universal, but opportunity is not.

The responsibility of opportunity.

Focus on the micro, and the macro takes care of itself.

Aubrey Marcus

Book: Own the day, own your life

Success is not something others can give you.

Darrin Donnelly

Book: Think like a warrior

Hierarchy-free and equal in contribution.

Nassim Nicholas Taleb

Book: Skin the game

When you are rewarded for perception, not results, you need to show sophistication.

Nassim Nicholas Taleb

Book: Skin the game

Thinking vs calculating.

You can tell if someone is really good at what they do by how specific they get.

If power corrupts, the reverse is also tru; persecution corrupts the victims, though perhaps in subtler and more tragic ways.

Koestler in Slavoj Zizek

Book: Violence

Paradigms die when they no longer fit the conditions of the real world.

George Gilder

Book: Life after Google

Gambling is only fraudulent when it is sold as an investment.

Tan Liu

Book: The ponzi factor

In business, the ability to conduct transactions is not optional. It is the way all economic learning and growth occurs. If your product is "free," it is not a product, and you are not in business, even if you can extort money from so-called advertisers to fund it.

George Gilder

Book: Life after Google

The thread today is no passivity, but pseudo-activity, the urge to 'be active', to 'participate', to mask the nothingness of what goes on.

Slavoj Zizek

Book: Violence

Until people realize that they are talking in a circle, however large that circle may be, they may continue to believe insinuations that give tautologies their power, as if they were conclusions about the external world instead of arbitrary definitions inside their own heads.

You never cure structural defects; the system corrects itself by collapsing.

Nassim Nicholas Taleb

Book: Skin the game

Calculation of opportunity costs can be a cost in its own right.

Richard Nisbett

Book: Mindware

Competition improves experience only as long as attention is focused primarily on the activity itself. If extrinsic goals -such as beating the opponent, wanting to impress an audience, or obtaining a big professional contract- are what one is concerned about, then competition is likely to become a distraction, rather than an incentive to focus consciousness on what is happening.

Business and Politics

Mihaly Csikszentmihaly

Book: Flow

The path of mastering something is the combination of not only doing the best you can do at it, but also it the best it can be done.

Gary Keller

Book: The ONE thing

Information is always available, but some is always silent.

Maria Kannikova

Book: Mastermind. How to Think Life Sherlock Holmes

A wealth of information creates a poverty of attention.

Herbert Simon

Book: Manage Your Day-to-Day

'The attitude of overinterpretation' is a self-cure for the fear of 'not getting it'.

Adam Phillips

Book: Missing out: In Praise of the Unlived Life

The hidden opportunity for a great comeback.

DC Gonzalez

Book: The Art of Mental Training

There is something claustrophobic in the life of a person wrapped up in their own little world.

Julian Baggini

Book: What's it all about?

Talent is universal, but opportunity is not.

Will this matter in 5 years?

"You need to unplug" assumes the default is plugged.

The largest impediment to thinking clearly about skill and luck is our innate desire to identify cause and effect.

Michael J. Mauboussin

Book: The success equation

Generosity is its own form of power.

>Frank Underwood
>
>TV-Series: House of cards

The problem with the terms is that they have been captured by dogmatists.

All ideals suffer in the confrontation with reality.

>Deng Ming-Dao
>
>Book: Scholar warrior

What, exactly, are the critical moves here?

Business and Politics

Daniel Coyle

Book: The little book of talent

The pain that accompanies a grand vision left unfulfilled.

Ashlee Vance

Book: Elon Musk

The paradox of skill: as skill improves, performance becomes more consistent, and therefore luck becomes more important.

Michael J. Mauboussin

Book: The success equation

Aid serves to generate further accumulation of capital in the advanced countries.

Slavoj Zizek

Book: Trouble in paradise

The principal biases of television news are not political at all. Rather, "the bias of the mainstream media is toward sensationalism, conflict and laziness".

Wallace in Jason Holt

Book: The ultimate Daily Show and philosophy

Nothing creates more stress than when our actions and behaviors aren't congruent with our values.

Darren Hardy

Book: The compound effect

The fatal temptation is to describe your market extremely narrowly so that you dominate it by definition.

Peter Thiel

Book: Zero to one

Politics is not about the surrendering of individual freedoms for the collective good but the surrendering of individual choices for the sake of collective freedom.

Julian Baggini

Power is a state of mind, work in, play in it, and stay in it.

Find canvases for other people to paint on. Be an anteambulo. Clear the path for the people above you and you will eventually create a patch for yourself.

Ryan Holiday
Book: Ego is the enemy

A focus on winning makes people focus outside themselves for validation of their worth.

Directional, not dogmatic.

Michael Hyatt and Daniel Harvaky

Book: Living forward

Money, of course, is still needed to survive, but time is what you need to live.

Rolf Potts

Book: Vagabonding

Business and Politics

About the author

Víctor de la Fuente, born in Barcelona in 1982, has an extensive professional career in the digital field while sport and travel have marked his philosophy of life.

On the professional side, the author has combined his core professional career with entrepreneurship and training. In his main job he has had the opportunity to work for companies of different sizes and nature such as Nestlé, Adevinta or Groupalia and Veepee to mention a few. To his main activity, he adds consulting services through his own agency vdelafuente where he collaborates with companies also from different sectors and with very different needs always in the field of digital marketing and eCommerce. In addition, Víctor de la Fuente actively collaborates with different universities such as the University of Barcelona, as well as different business schools such as MIOTI or ISDI, among others, as a professor in different masters and postgraduate courses. In his professional career, he also has experience as an entrepreneur co-founding, among others, a fashion application in startup mode along with two other founders.

On the personal side, Victor de la Fuente's life is marked mainly by a trip around the world where he carried only a backpack for 7 months. His life is also marked by his dedication to sports, especially running, where he has participated in numerous marathons and mountain ultramarathons. All this has given him a unique vision of life mixing stoicism, Buddhism and essentialism, among other philosophies.

Other books by the author

Published in English:

- 365 quotes and meditations. English version. Víctor de la Fuente. 2021
- Against utopía. English version. Víctor de la Fuente. 2022
- Digital detox. English version. Víctor de la Fuente. 2020
- Minimalism: live better with less (and achieve mental quietness). English version. Víctor de la Fuente. 2016
- Poems from a metal heart. English version. Víctor de la Fuente. 2021
- Smart Simple Investment Strategy. English version. Víctor de la Fuente. 2021
- Stoicism and Zen Buddhism in Modern Life. English version. Víctor de la Fuente. 2023

Publicados en castellano:

- Aprende a Invertir. Versión en castellano. Víctor de la Fuente. 2021
- Ciberacoso: un problema IRL. Versión en castellano. Víctor de la Fuente. 2023
- Contra la utopía. Versión en castellano. Víctor de la Fuente. 2022
- Detox digital. Versión en castellano. Víctor de la Fuente. 2020
- Estoicismo y budismo zen en la vida moderna. Versión en castellano. Víctor de la Fuente. 2023
- La estrategia win y otros ensayos de la economía digital. Versión en castellano. Víctor de la Fuente. 2023
- Minimalismo: vivir mejor con menos y lograr calma mental. Versión en castellano. Víctor de la Fuente. 2016